Stepping Stones

Meditations and Prayers for Spiritual Renewal

by

Cecile Bauer

De La Salle House

Paulist Press
New York/Mahwah, N.J.

Cover design by Kokopelli Design Studio

Library of Congress Cataloging-in-Publication Data

Bauer, Cecile.
    Stepping stones : meditations and prayers for spiritual renewal / by Cecile Bauer.
        p. cm.
    ISBN 0-8091-3916-2 (alk. paper)
    1. Bible Meditations. 2. Bible—Devotional use.
3. Bible—Prayers. I. Title.
BS491.5.B38 1999
242′.5—dc21   99-40902
                                                         CIP

Published by Paulist Press
997 Macarthur Boulevard
Mahwah, New Jersey 07430

www.paulistpress.com

Printed and bound in the
United States of America

Contents

Introduction   1

Chapters:

1   **Hearts of Stone**   3
Ezekiel 36

2   **Jacob's Stone Pillow**   6
Genesis 28

3   **Water from Stone**   9
Exodus 17

4   **Diseased Stones**   12
Leviticus 14

5   **Written in Stone**   15
Deuteronomy 5

6   **Altar Stones**   18
Deuteronomy 27

7   **The Twelve Stones of Jordan**   20
Joshua 3 and 4

 8 **Stones from the Sky**   23
    Joshua 10

 9 **Small Stones of Courage**   26
    1 Samuel 17

10 **Stones Thrown in Anger**   29
    2 Samuel 16

11 **Absalom's Pile of Stones**   32
    2 Samuel 18 and 19

12 **Solomon's Temple Stones**   35
    1 Kings 6

13 **Elijah's Stone Altar**   38
    1 Kings 18

14 **Joram's Stone Fields**   42
    2 Kings 3

15 **Stones of Job**   45
    Job 1 and 6

16 **Stones of Hopelessness**   48
    Job 14

17 **The Leviathan Heart of Stone**   50
    Job 40 and 41

18 **Scatter/Gather Stones**   53
    Ecclesiastes 1 and 3

19 **Born Again Stones**   56
    Matthew 3 and Luke 3

20 **Temptation Stones**   **59**
    Matthew 4

21 **Pride Stones**   **62**
    Matthew 4

22 **Stumbling Stones**   **65**
    Luke 7

23 **Stone Water Jars**   **68**
    John 2

24 **Stones of Denial**   **71**
    Matthew 7 and Luke 11

25 **Millstones**   **74**
    Mark 9 and Matthew 18

26 **Judgment Stones**   **77**
    John 10

27 **Vanity Stones**   **80**
    Matthew 24

28 **Weapon Stones**   **83**
    Mark 5

29 **Singing Stones**   **86**
    Luke 19

30 **Building Stones**   **89**
    Luke 19

31 **Cornerstone/Keystone**   **92**
    Matthew 21 and Isaiah 28

32 Pretty Stones 95
Luke 21

33 Punishing Stones 98
John 8

34 Stones of Darkness 101
John 11

35 A Stone's Throw 104
Luke 22

36 Stones of Despair 107
Matthew 27

37 Seal the Stone 110
Matthew 27

38 Unseal the Stone 113
Matthew 28

39 The Stoning of Stephen 116
Acts 7

40 Living Stones 119
1 Peter 2 and 5

Introduction

Stepping Stones is a collection of stories taken from the Old and New Testament. Each chapter uses stones in a different way as a symbol of faith. Parts of the book have been discussed during my group scripture study at St. Mary's Church in Crown, Pennsylvania. These stories, prayers, and meditations were written to encourage a renewed interest in reading the Bible.

A special thank-you to my pastor and mentor, Father Thomas Hoderny of St. Mary's. Without Father Tom's encouragement and spiritual direction, this book may never have been completed. Also, I am grateful to Father Gerald Ryle, pastor of St. Lawrence Church in North Highlands, California. Father Jerry opened my mind and heart to the continuing journey of scripture study.

Chapter 1
Hearts of Stone

> **The word of the Lord came to Ezekiel: "I will give you a new heart and place a new spirit within you, taking from your bodies your hearts of stone and giving you natural hearts...You shall be my people and I will be your God."**
>
> **Ezekiel 36:26, 28**

Ezekiel, an Old Testament priest and prophet during the Babylonian exile, is sometimes called the father of Judaism. His heavenly visions and prophecies helped reestablish the covenant between God and the exiled people of Jerusalem. Punished because of their sins and hardened hearts, they were conquered and deported by King Nebuchadnezzar around 597 B.C. This King of Babylon destroyed the temple ten years later. Only when the Jewish nation relented and turned back to God were they allowed to return to the Promised Land and rebuild the temple.

Has sin hardened us to the word of God? Does our faith feel cold, like a stone in our hearts? What would it take to turn our stony hearts into warm, feeling, natural hearts again? Ezekiel urged his people to turn their hearts to God. Who will be our prophet today? Does a special liturgy, a homily, speak to us? When we give a sign of peace to our neighbor, do we truly wish to spread peace, or is it just an empty gesture? Do we allow the warm hug of a friend to melt away some of our indifference? Is Jesus knocking on the stony gates of our hearts? How do we respond?

Read Ezekiel, Chapter 37. This powerful vision of the field of bones restored to life by the Spirit of God is sometimes read at liturgies during the Vigil of Pentecost.

> **"...I prophesied as he told me, and the spirit came into them; they came alive and stood upright, a vast army...."**
> **Ezekiel 37:10**

The images in the field-of-bones story always bring a shiver of awe to me. How powerful is our Creator, that he can take dead bones and restore them to life again! God will also restore the dead places in our faith if we open our hearts to his grace. Our faith journey is meant to change stony hearts into the living stones of faith. Stand upright for the

Lord! Pray that our loving Father in heaven will place a new spirit within us.

Heavenly Father, help us today. Dead in sin, we have become hardened and heartless to the needs of others. Forgive us for the times we turned away from you and your message of love. Replace our hearts of stone with warm, natural hearts. In Jesus' name we pray. Amen.

Chapter 2
Jacob's Stone Pillow

Jacob, who later became the leader of the nation Israel, had a checkered past. This man of the Old Testament was the second born of twin sons to Isaac and Rebekah. Early Jewish law intended that the father's inheritance should go to the oldest son, Esau. The patriarch Isaac, old and blind, was easily deceived by Jacob and Rebekah. He blessed his younger son Jacob by mistake. Worried that the eldest son, Esau would kill his deceitful brother, Rebekah sent Jacob off to her brother's family in Haran. While on his journey, Jacob encountered God.

> **Jacob departed from Beer-sheba and proceeded toward Haran. When he came upon a certain shrine, as the sun had already set, he stopped there for the night. Taking one of the stones from the shrine, he put it under his head and lay down to sleep at that spot. Then he had a dream: a**

stairway rested on the ground, with its top reaching to the heavens, and God's messengers were going up and down on it. And there was the LORD standing beside him and saying:

"I, the LORD, am the God of your forefather Abraham and the God of Isaac; the land on which you are lying I will give to you and your descendants...Know that I am with you; I will protect you wherever you go, and bring you back to this land...."

Genesis 28:10–15

A stone pillow brings to mind tough times. It reminds us of homeless people looking for rest and comfort, with nothing to rest their weary heads on except unyielding stone sidewalks. Jacob, forced to leave his comfortable home because of his own treachery, must now wander in a strange land. Yet, God does not forget the deceitful Jacob. Nor does he forget other homeless or hopeless people. He loves us all and wants only good things for us.

The vision of Jacob's stairway to heaven gives hope to all those looking to God for a helping hand with daily problems. Sometimes we only need a little encouragement to lift us from our despair. A caring friend offers food, or listens to our worries. A job opportunity helps ease staggering debt. We dream of God, and awaken with tears of joy. No matter how hard the stone pillow beneath our heads, God promises,

> **"…I am with you; I will protect you wherever you go…."**
> **Genesis 28:15**

Pray that we will never fall into despair so deep that we cannot turn to God for help.

God of our ancestors, keep us safe this night. When our pillows of stone seem too hard to bear, lift us up. Keep us alert to your messengers who bring hope and comfort in the dark nights of our soul. In Jesus' name we pray. Amen.

Chapter 3
Water from Stone

During the Exodus from Egypt, the Chosen People wandered in the desert—a dry, waterless place.

> **From the desert of Sin the whole Israelite community journeyed by stages, as the LORD directed, and encamped at Rephidim. Here there was no water for the people to drink.**
>
> **Exodus 17:1**

When the going gets tough, what do the people of God do? They quarrel, grumble, and complain. They questioned their leader, Moses:

> **"...Why did you ever make us leave Egypt? Was it just to have us die here of thirst with our children and our livestock?" So Moses cried out to the LORD, "What shall I do**

with this people? A little more and they will stone me!"

Exodus 17:3, 4

God directed Moses to take his staff, the same staff that parted the Red Sea, and strike a large stone with the staff:

"...Strike the rock, and the water will flow from it for the people to drink...."

Exodus 17:6

In *Bible Stories,* a textbook used in the classrooms of my youth, this scene shares a detail from Numbers 20:11: Moses struck the rock once and nothing happened. As the thirsty people grumbled against God, Moses struck the rock a second time. Because he doubted God's word, Moses was denied entrance into the Promised Land. God instructed him to train Joshua to be the new leader of the people (Nm 27).

The story of water gushing from the desert stone still inspires present-day believers. Our God is a god of miracles. Even parched rock will yield life-giving water to those who believe. Souls parched by dry years of unbelief can drink of the life-giving water of Christ's love. All we need is faith and trust. Let us pray that our Creator will touch the stony places in our hearts and bring forth fresh, clear, life-renewing strength.

O God, you created life from the dry desert stones. Keep us in your loving care as we struggle on our journey to your promised reward. When the journey gets tough, teach us not to grumble against your will. You will answer when the time is right for us. As always, we make our prayer in Jesus' name. Amen.

Chapter 4
Diseased Stones

Leviticus, the third book of the Old Testament, consists of ritual laws prescribed for the priests of the tribe of Levi. These laws served to teach the Israelites that they should always keep themselves in a state of purity, or legal sanctity, as a sign of their intimate union with God.

Several chapters deal with leprosy, the dreaded "unclean" disease of that time. The priests were required to judge not only true leprosy, but any suspicious pimple, boil, burn scar—even a man's loss of hair. All skin irregularities were considered portents of leprosy. Not only were victims of leprosy forbidden to approach other people, but they were exiled outside the camp. Their clothing and dwellings were also considered unclean. Any person or any item that had touched chair, bed, clothing, food—even the living quarters "contaminated" by a leper—was also considered unclean. Shunned, hungry, and ultimately homeless, the victims of leprosy were reduced to begging. Almost half of Chapter 14 deals with leprosy of houses:

> ...If a leprous infection [occurs] on any house...the owner shall come and report it to the priest....If he finds that the infection has spread on the walls, he shall order the infected stones to be pulled out and cast in an unclean place outside the city. [Later]...if [the priest] finds that the infection has spread...it shall be pulled down, and all its stones, beams and mortar shall be hauled away to an unclean place outside the city.
>
> Leviticus 14:33–45

Who are the lepers of today's world? What group of unfortunate people do we shun and turn away from? Drug and alcohol addicts, the homeless, persons with AIDS, even cancer patients, are avoided as if their afflictions were "catching."

In ancient times, what might have been an attack of mildew on the walls of a stucco house caused the entire home to be demolished—an extreme example of ritual cleanliness. Today's homeowner, confronted with a dark discoloration on the walls, would reach for a bottle of bleach. Who would be fanatical enough to dismantle their home because of mildew and discard it on a dump outside the city?

How do we react to modern-day "uncleanliness"? As Christians, what is our reaction to the misfortune of others? Do we refuse to allow a halfway house to exist in our neighborhood? Have we ignored the outstretched hand of a present-day beggar? Do we silently applaud the burning down of an abortion clinic? Remember the words of Jesus that we are not to judge, lest we be found wanting! May we never be found guilty of tearing down the hopes and dreams of others.

O God, you see the hearts of all your children. Temper our tendency to judge others to be unclean. You alone are judge of the universe. Teach us to be part of the solution for the social evils of our days. Wash our hearts clean that we may serve you by helping others. As always, we pray in Jesus' name. Amen.

Chapter 5
Written in Stone

God rescued the Israelite people from years of bondage in Egypt. As they neared the Promised Land, God met Moses on the mountain at Horeb. He spoke to him from the midst of the fire.

> Moses summoned all Israel and said to them, "Hear, O Israel, the statutes and decrees which I proclaim in your hearing this day, that you may learn them and take care to observe them. The LORD, our God, made a covenant with us at Horeb; not with our fathers did he make this covenant, but with us, all of us who are alive here this day."
>
> Deuteronomy 5:1–3

After proclaiming to the Israelites the ten commandments of the Covenant, Moses said to them:

> "These words, and nothing more, the LORD spoke with a loud voice to your entire

assembly on the mountain from the midst of the fire and the dense cloud. He wrote them upon two tablets of stone and gave them to me."

Deuteronomy 5:22

The Ten Commandments, basic moral laws that are still relevant today, were written on tablets of stone. These commandments were handed down from God to Moses and thence to the people of Israel (and through Jesus, to us).

Early scribes wrote on stone to preserve history or words of wisdom. Parchment, an early form of paper, was also used for correspondence. But really important messages were "written in stone." It must have been a long, time-consuming art, chiseling words on stone. The very nature of these early "books" meant them to be indestructible, permanent records to be handed down through the ages. Written in stone still means an unchangeable law or rule.

The Israelites had been brought out of the land of their captivity by God, rescued from the Red Sea, and fed manna in the desert. Now, approaching the Promised Land, God offered them a Covenant, written in stone. But the ancient books of the Bible tell us that these same Israelites soon turned away from their God. While Moses lingered on the mountain top in union with God, the people grew restless.

Afraid Moses had died, leaving them without a leader, they melted their gold jewelry, built a golden calf and worshiped it. In frustrated anger, Moses flung the stone tablets on the ground, breaking them. The stone tablets broke, but the Covenant between God and his people remains.

Are we like the early children of God? Do we believe for a time, then turn away when something happens to frighten us? Have we forgotten all the miracles God does for us every day? When things go wrong, do we turn to the golden calves of the quick fix? Do we try to forget our problems with chemical comfort? Do we fling down the stones of our Covenant with God, our trust and belief in his golden mercy? Let us pray that we will have the strength to endure hardship, to be stone-like in our faith.

O God of the Covenant, teach us to be faithful to your laws. When we become tempted by the golden calves of modern-day distractions, comfort us with your enduring presence. In Jesus' name we pray. Amen.

Chapter 6
Altar Stones

Moses gave his final instructions to the people before they crossed the Jordan into the Promised Land. He gave this order:

> ...you shall also build to the LORD, your God, an altar made of stones that no iron tool has touched.
>
> **Deuteronomy 27:5**

Why was the altar built of undressed stones? Did the God most high disdain the handiwork of his humans? Or did the moving and setting up of natural stones prove to be more difficult? Perhaps it took more time and patience to find just the right flat stones for an altar. But a more likely explanation was the commandment against false idols. God knew that the Israelites lived in captivity in pagan Egypt, and were taught to worship their pagan gods. The first of the Ten Commandments given to Moses warned:

"I, the LORD am your God...You shall not have other gods beside me. You shall not carve idols for yourselves...."

Deuteronomy 5:6

For people trained to worship idols, any flat stone may have cried out to be carved into something beautiful. The pagan gods were many: earth and sea, sky and wind, stars and clouds, earthquakes, volcanic eruptions—any natural or unnatural phenomenon, was considered to be a god. Pagan people believed they must appease these multiple gods by carving images and worshiping them. Perhaps to avoid this temptation to idolatry in his beloved chosen people, God ordered only undressed stones used for his altars.

What are our idols today? What earthly thing or things do we worship instead of giving all honor to our Creator God? New car? Motor Home? Bigger house? State of the art TV or computer? What owns us? Who or what is carved on our hearts? Let us pray that our Creator will always remain first in our hearts.

O God of creation, teach us to give all honor and glory to you. Restrain our earthly appetites for newer, bigger, brighter idols, for you alone are our God; you alone are worthy of our worship. In Jesus' name we pray. Amen.

Chapter 7
The Twelve Stones of Jordan

After they wandered in the desert for forty years, the entire nation of Israel prepared to cross into the Promised Land. The Lord instructed Joshua to have priests carry the Ark of the Covenant into the Jordan river.

> No sooner had these priestly bearers of the
> Ark waded into the waters at the edge of
> the Jordan, which overflows all its banks
> during the entire season of the harvest, than
> the waters flowing from upstream halted,
> backing up in a solid mass for a very great
> distance...while those flowing
> downstream...disappeared entirely. Thus
> the people crossed over opposite Jericho.
>
> ### Joshua 3:15, 16

This miraculous crossing of the Israelites, often overshadowed by Moses' parting of the Red Sea, marks their entrance into the Promised Land. The Lord gave additional orders that day:

> ...the LORD said to Joshua, "Choose twelve men from the people, one from each tribe, and instruct them to take up twelve stones from this spot in the bed of the Jordan where the priests have been standing motionless. Carry them over with you, and place them where you are to stay tonight."
>
> Joshua 4:1–3

Joshua gave the order. He told his men:

> ...lift to your shoulders one stone apiece...In the future, these are to be a sign among you. When your children ask you what these stones mean to you, you shall answer them, "The waters of the Jordan ceased to flow before the Ark of the Covenant of the LORD when it crossed the Jordan." Thus these stones are to serve as a perpetual memorial.
>
> Joshua 4:5–7

Why are these memorial stones important to modern-day believers? The Israelites were nomads for forty years. They traveled light, carrying their few possessions with them, and relied on the Lord for food and drink to sustain them. Now the Lord wanted them to lift to their shoulders large stones from the river bed to make a memorial to his covenant. The memorial stones served as an eternal reminder of the passage through the Jordan river. Perhaps the stones were also a symbol of the permanence of their new home, the promised land flowing with milk and honey.

What are our memorials of the Lord's promise? In Jesus, the cross and resurrection serve to remind us of our Savior's promise of eternal life in him. Every time we gaze at a crucifix, every time we make the sign of the cross, every time we receive the Eucharist, we remember. Let us pray that we never forget our Lord's promises.

O Jesus, remind us of your covenant with your people. We do not need memorial stones, or a land filled with milk and honey, to gain eternal life in you. Your love and your loving way of life are all the examples we need to cross over to eternal happiness. Sustain us on our journey to you, O Lord, our rock and salvation. Amen.

Chapter 8
Stones from the Sky

Joshua, the successor of Moses, led the Israelite nation across the Jordan into their Promised Land. The inhabitants of Canaan did not give up their land without a fight. After they defeated the people of Jericho, Joshua and his soldiers challenged the five Amorite kings.

> **And when Joshua made his surprise attack upon them...the LORD threw them into disorder before him...While they fled before Israel along the descent from Beth-horon, the LORD hurled great stones from the sky above them all the way to Azekah, killing many. More died from these hailstones than the Israelites slew with the sword.**
>
> **Joshua 10:9–11**

The Old Testament is full of examples of God as a holy warrior. The great stones hurled down from the sky enhanced the image of God as a punishing deity.

Earthquakes, tornadoes, tidal waves, volcanoes, cancers, AIDS, are punishment from God, some mistakenly believe. "God's will," we say, when disasters happen to strangers. When someone we love is stricken, the killing stones may overwhelm us. Sometimes we wonder what great sin we are guilty of to bring down the wrath of God from the sky. It is not easy to say, "Let God's will be done," as we hold a dying loved one in our arms. We wonder why and wail aloud against the Warrior God who inflicts such pain on his lowly critters.

But Jesus gave us a new image of God: Abba, Daddy, with all the love and comfort those human terms bring to mind. We were created in the image of God. Would a loving father deliberately cause pain and suffering to his precious children? What if we were guilty of great wrong and in need of punishment?

What about the innocent ones who seem to suffer most from unexplained "stones from the sky." What about young children left behind when their parents die? What sins have AIDS babies committed? How about the victims of wars and natural disasters?

Tough questions need extra prayer. We will not know the answers until the final days. Many Christians believe that God weeps with us as we struggle to come to terms with tragedy. Let us pray that he will strengthen us each day, especially during times of trial.

Abba, God, you who are our Father and Creator, strengthen us as we struggle through the tough times. Teach us to rely on your wisdom, your will for us. Guard and protect us and our loved ones, now and at the hour of our deaths. In Jesus' name we pray. Amen.

Chapter 9
Small Stones of Courage

When the great King Saul engaged in battle with the army of Philistines, a giant named Goliath challenged the army of Israel. For forty days and nights, the giant insulted Saul's men. None of the soldiers was brave enough to go into battle with the giant. David, who would later become the greatest king of Israel (and who was Jesus' ancestor), was then a young shepherd boy, tending sheep for his father, Jesse. Sent to the army camp to deliver food to his brothers, David heard the boasts of Goliath and said:

> **...Who is this...Philistine...that he should insult the armies of the living God?**
> **1 Samuel 17:26**

Sent to King Saul, David volunteered to fight Goliath. Saul put a bronze helmet on the boy's head and clothed him in a coat of mail. But David found the armor too heavy and cumbersome, so he removed it.

> Then, staff in hand, David selected five
> smooth stones from the wadi [ravine] and
> put them in the pocket of his shepherd's
> bag. With his sling also ready...he
> approached the Philistine.
>
> 1 Samuel 17:40

As Goliath noticed the youngster approaching him
with staff in hand, he laughed and roared more
threats and insults.

> David answered him: "You come against me
> with sword and spear and scimitar, but I
> come against you in the name of the LORD
> of hosts...Today the LORD shall deliver you
> into my hand...For the battle is the LORD's,
> and he shall deliver you into our hands."
>
> 1 Samuel 17:45–47

So with five small stones, a shepherd boy defeats
an evil giant. But it was not David's strength or the
small stones that bought the victory, but his faith in
the God of Israel.

Will our faith strengthen us in our daily battles
against wickedness? What are the evil giants in our
day? Prejudice, injustice, homelessness, hunger,
abortion, the Right to Die? What can we do with the
small stones of our faith? Stones flung at a problem
will not solve it. But an open hand, extended to help

others, may perform miracles. Daily prayer, the small stones we offer to our God, may not seem important to us. To God, it is proof of our faith, our trust in him. Prayer joined with social action (such as helping at soup kitchens, donating clothing, sending post-cards to Congress to repeal the abortion act) are the small daily stones that will eventually bring God's will to fruition in our lives. **For the battle is the Lord's.** Pray that the Lord's will be done.

O God, you who strengthened the boy David as he challenged an evil giant, strengthen us today. We need your wisdom and strength as we battle the evil of our days. Teach us to rely on you, O Lord of Hosts, not on our own feeble weapons, our small stones of righteousness. In Jesus' name we pray. Amen.

Chapter 10
Stones Thrown in Anger

The Old Testament's Second book of Samuel describes David's ascent to kingship. It is full of accounts of war and treachery, families divided, brother killing brother. Even Absalom, the son of King David, murdered his brother and plotted to kill his father, the king. At one point David was forced to flee the armies of Absalom, leaving Jerusalem and hiding in the surrounding hills.

As David approached Bahurim, a man related to the previous king, Saul, came out of the place,

> ...cursing as he came. He threw stones at David and at all the king's officers, even though all the soldiers, including the royal guard, were on David's right and on his left.
>
> **2 Samuel 16:5, 6**

The guards and soldiers became outraged at this insult to their king. One called the tormentor a dead

dog and sought permission to "lop off his head."
David denied the request. Instead the king said...

> **"If my own son, who came forth from my
> loins, is seeking my life, how much more
> might this Benjaminite do so? Let him alone
> and let him curse, for the LORD has told him
> to. Perhaps the LORD will look upon my
> affliction and make it up to me with benefits
> for the curses he is uttering this day."**
>
> **2 Samuel 16:11, 12**

This scene reveals much about David's compassion. His heart must have been breaking at the thought of his own son seeking his life. Earlier, Absalom had murdered his brother, fled into exile for three years, then sought, and received, the king's forgiveness. Now, after gathering an army, David's oldest son sought to murder his father and become king himself. The pesky man hurling stones at David's royal guard might have seemed like the last straw to a beleaguered king. Instead, David forgives him, and allows the stone throwing to continue!

What lesson can modern-day Christians learn from an ancient biblical king? Patience under trial. Forgiveness of pesky enemies. Prudence as we look to our heavenly Father for justice. Jesus taught many lessons about forgiveness: turn the other cheek; if an enemy takes your coat, give him your cloak as well;

forgive seven times seventy. Tough lessons in today's dog-eat-dog world. What if a co-worker puts you down? Or if a family member gossips about your children? Or if a neighbor curses and throws stones at your dog? Let them alone; let them curse. The Lord will make it up to us for our affliction. Let God act as the avenging angel. Pray that today's stones, flung in anger, will fail to stir us to reciprocal rage.

O God, protect us from stones flung in anger. Teach us to heed the example of King David and Jesus. For it is not flung stones that kill our souls, but the sin of revenge. In Jesus' name we pray. Amen.

Chapter 11
Absalom's Pile of Stones

Events did not go well for Absalom, son of King David, as his army neared David's troops. Absalom's Commander, Joab, deserted and went over to serve the king. The youth's advisors quarreled over attack plans. One hung himself. So intent was Absalom on victory over the existing king, that he seemed blind to the direction he traveled. He rode a mule under the branches of a large terebinth—a thorny tree with tangled branches. The youth's long hair became caught in the limbs. Absalom hung between heaven and earth while the mule ran off. Imagine his roaring anger, this man who wished to become king, as he swung by the hair, helpless. His armor and sword were futile before the power of God.

Joab, his former officer, finding Absalom hanging so helplessly, killed him with pikes, then called all the armies to a halt.

Absalom was taken up and cast into a deep pit in the forest, and a very large mound of stones was erected over him....

2 Samuel 18:17

King David mourned his wicked son's death.

"My son Absalom! My son, my son Absalom! If only I had died instead of you...."

2 Samuel 19:1

No matter that the youth tried to kill him and steal his throne, David loved Absalom and wept for him. He flung himself into such a state of mourning that his advisors feared for his sanity. One questioned why the king wept for his son, when his kingdom needed him to be a strong leader and unite the people. So David put mourning behind him for the good of his people.

Would we have such a strong love as to mourn for a son intent upon murdering us? Family ties go deep, yet would we mourn a renegade child who seems to be pure evil? What would we do in such circumstances? Jesus tells us to forgive. Why is it so difficult to forgive those whom we love? Perhaps because we expect our loved ones not to hurt us but to love us. When they fail to do so, do we harden our hearts? As we swing, helpless, between heaven and earth, is it possible to forgive true evil?

Remember, no matter how sinful or wicked we, or our loved ones, may be, our heavenly Father weeps for us too. God forgives us many more times than David forgave his son. No matter how high we pile the stones of sin over us, God will never forget us. Pray that we will always remember our heavenly Father's kind and forgiving love.

O heavenly Father, forgive us for the times we doubted your loving nature. Teach us to return to you when our human ambition leads us astray. For no matter how heinous our mistakes, our lofty ambitions, our sins of greed, you always love and forgive us. Thank you, Father, for being our refuge in times of trouble. In Jesus' name we pray. Amen.

Chapter 12
Solomon's Temple Stones

After the death of King David, his son Solomon became king. In the fourth year of his reign over Israel (968 B.C.), Solomon began the construction of a temple dedicated to the Lord. For a detailed description of the building of this beautiful temple, read 1 Kings 6:1–38. Because this is a study of stone stories, we will concentrate on verse 7:

> **The temple was built of stone dressed at the quarry, so that no hammer, axe, or iron tool was to be heard in the temple during its construction.**
>
> **1 Kings 6:7**

Why did King Solomon, or his construction overseer, command that the sound of stonecutters not be allowed in the temple? Surely the building site echoed with the varied noises of normal construction? Workers, wrestling to fit heavy blocks of stone into place, must have groaned under their burdens. Oxen, dragging cedar timbers, must have snorted and pawed the ground as they labored. Why did they ban the sound of stone being chiseled into large blocks? Does the Creator—who made thunder, earthquakes, tornadoes and other noisy natural wonders—really prefer silence? Or was it humans who banned noise in the temple? Who can understand the mind-set of ancient kings? Who really knows the mind of God?

Before the reforms of Vatican II, Catholics attended mass in silence. Only priests and altar servers were allowed to speak or sing (in hushed tones barely heard by the congregation). The faithful were to *hear* mass, not pray aloud.

Some other Christian churches valued silence as well. Yet Southern Baptist congregations have a long history of enthusiastic singing, joyful responses, swaying and clapping, as they celebrate their faith. Some people are made uncomfortable by the Baptists' fervor, while others among us admire their exuberant liturgies and their courage to shout out their faith!

Is there any one right way to worship our Creator?

Catholics have come a long way since Vatican II. Now mass is truly a celebration! Joyful hymns enliven the mass. People are encouraged to respond aloud with songs, prayers and petitions. Unfortunately today, as in Solomon's day, many people still cling to silent worship. Falsely bound by ancient laws, they sit in stony silence. Many still refuse to "sing a joyful noise unto the Lord." We who enjoy singing are not to judge them, but to pray that their hearts (and mouths) will be opened.

O God of silence and of joyful noise, open up our stony hearts to you. We want to do your will, O Lord, in all things. Teach us not to judge the faith of others, especially their forms of worshiping you. In Jesus' name we pray. Amen.

Chapter 13
Elijah's Stone Altar

After the death of King Solomon, the Israelites drifted away from serving the one true God and began, instead, to worship the pagan god Baal. During the reign of Ahab there arose a great prophet, Elijah the Tishbite. Elijah warned King Ahab to reform his ways or the Lord would withhold rain and the people would starve. Forced to flee for his life, Elijah moved east of the Jordan and hid near a stream. Ravens brought him bread and meat, morning and evening, for a year.

In the third year of the drought, the Lord sent Elijah to confront King Ahab. The king, at Elijah's direction, summoned all Israel, and hundreds of prophets of Baal, to assemble on Mount Carmel. Each prophet planned to demonstrate the power of his gods.

> **Elijah appealed to all the people and said, "How long will you straddle the issue? If**

**the LORD is God, follow him, if Baal, follow
him."** The people, however, did not answer
him. So Elijah said to the people, "I am the
only surviving prophet of the LORD and
there are four hundred and fifty prophets of
Baal. Give us two young bulls [to be
burned for sacrifice]....You shall call on
your gods, and I will call on the LORD. The
God who answers with fire is God." All the
people answered, "Agreed!"

1 Kings 18:21–24

The prophets of Baal prepared their bull for sacrifice and placed it on their altar. But although they danced around it, called loudly to their god, and even slashed themselves with swords and spears, no fire rained down from Baal.

**But there was not a sound; no one
answered, and no one was listening.**

1 Kings 18:29

Elijah called the people to him. He repaired the altar of the Lord that had been destroyed. He took twelve stones, for the number of tribes of the sons of Jacob, and built an altar in honor of the Lord. Elijah also dug a trench around the altar.

**When he had arranged the wood, he cut up
the young bull and laid it on the wood.**

39

> "Fill four jars with water," he said, "and pour it over the holocaust and over the wood." " Do it again," he said, and they did it again. "Do it a third time."...The water flowed around the altar, and the trench was filled with the water.

> 1 Kings 18:33–35

Elijah prayed to the Lord.

> "Answer me, LORD! Answer me, that this people may know that you, LORD are God...." The LORD's fire came down and consumed the holocaust, wood, stones, and dust, and it lapped up the water in the trench. Seeing this, all the people fell prostrate and said, "The LORD is God! The LORD is God!"

> 1 Kings 18:37–39

How much does it take to turn our hearts from false gods? False gods invade our lives every day. The false god of immorality is casually flaunted in magazines, movies, on TV and over the Internet. Power is a false god. Politicians, seeking election, promise to effect a real reform in government. Once elected, "the people's choice" often fails to keep election promises. The false god of materialism snags most of us. The push for new things—automobiles, houses, designer clothing, recreational vehicles—plunges too many households into serious debt. A once-popular song beseeches, "Oh Lord, won't you buy me a Mercedes-Benz?" A modern version of Elijah's words, "Answer me, Lord! Answer me!"

So how do we pour water over our burning desire for more things, more power, more pleasure? What can we offer to our God in return for his everlasting love? Should we place our hard-earned things on a stone altar and call down fire from God to consume them? A dramatic idea, but is it what God really wants of us? Perhaps, like the fallen away tribes of Israel, the God of love is calling us back to simple faith. He wants us to offer service to others, as a way of living out our faith in him. Pray that we can put aside our false gods and live simple lives of faith and trust.

O Lord of all, hear our plea. Teach us how best to serve you in these troubled times. May our sacrifices of time and talent in the service of others, and our prayer, ignite the fire of faith in all of us, your followers. In Jesus' name we pray. Amen.

Chapter 14
Joram's Stone Fields

After the death of Ahab, his son Joram became king of Israel. Second Kings, Chapter 3, describes Joram, his sins against the Lord and the campaign [war] he waged against Mesha the king of Moab. Elisha, the prophet who succeeded Elijah, called upon the Lord to help Joram's armies win the war.

> The power of the LORD came upon Elisha and he announced, "Thus says the LORD...[I] will deliver Moab into your grasp. You shall destroy every fortified city, fell every fruit tree, stop up all the springs, and ruin every fertile field with stones."
>
> **2 Kings 3:15–19**

This seems like a very harsh punishment against the territory of Moab. It was not enough to conquer the people, but their means of providing food and water were also destroyed. Filling a fertile field with stones meant months of work for the conquered people to remove the stones before they could begin to plant again. They would also need to dig out their water supply and plant more fruit trees to feed their people. Perhaps God meant to keep the warrior people so busy with basic survival that they would not have the time nor the energy to continue fighting his will for their lives.

The Old Testament God often seems cruel and vengeful. What we cannot know is how evil the Moab people were to bring down such a wretched punishment upon themselves. As in the story of Sodom and Gomorrah, God punished evil with dramatic finality. Many people today still regard the Creator as harsh and punitive. Our lives may go terribly wrong: the death of a beloved one, downsizing at work, homes lost to foreclosure, abject poverty, crippling accidents, cancer or incurable diseases. Do we then blame the Old Testament vengeful God? *(We have to blame **somebody**, God!)*

Yet, our heavenly Father has a plan. Every crisis in our lives, once overcome, may help to strengthen us. Jesus taught us about our loving Father, Abba (daddy). Perhaps God wants to shake up our lives in order to teach us valuable lessons. Like the hapless Moabites, forced to concentrate on basic survival instead of waging war, will we learn from our tragedies? Or will we continue to fight God's plan for our lives? Each of us, every day, needs to pray for acceptance of God's will for us.

O God, Creator, master of all things in heaven and on earth, teach us to rely on your will. We need to see your beloved hand in our lives as we struggle through the tough times. Your Son taught us to call you Abba. Be a beloved Father to us all. In Jesus' name we pray. Amen.

Chapter 15
Stones of Job

The Old Testament story of Job tells the story of a just man's desire to understand why bad things happen to good people.

> **In the land of Uz there was a blameless and upright man named Job, who feared God and avoided evil. Seven sons and three daughters were born to him; and he had seven thousand sheep, three thousand camels, five hundred yoke of oxen, five hundred she-asses, and a great number of work animals, so that he was greater than any of the men of the East.**
>
> **Job 1:1–3**

God allowed the devil to tempt Job's faith. Everything he owned was destroyed, including his children. Horrible boils covered his body. His wife encouraged him to curse God and die. Even though he fell into despair, Job's faith persevered. Three friends came to console Job. Their conversations and advice, and Job's anguished responses, make up the Book of Job. He answers his friend Eliphaz:

> "...I have not transgressed the commands of the Holy One. / What strength have I that I should endure, / and what is my limit that I should be patient? / Have I the strength of stones, or is my flesh of bronze? / Have I no helper...?"

Job 6:10–13

Job's lament strikes a chord with any person who has suffered through a terrible crisis. It is human nature to look for answers, and to blame God for our problems. Who among us has not shaken his or her fist at the sky when someone dear to us dies unexpectedly? When a child is horribly injured by evil people? When our homes, or jobs, or families are swept away by freakish weather or natural disasters? It shakes our faith when terrible things happen. Like Job, we question God.

How could you let this happen, God? And why? What have I done to deserve this? Give me a break, God! I'm not made of stone, you know.

The book of Job is excellent reading for those struggling with overwhelming problems in their own lives. Job's conversations with his friends, his questioning of God, and God's answers, often strike a chord in the hearts of troubled people. Let us pray that we will never fall into despair and that our faith, like Job's, will survive any trial.

O God, you who designed the heavens and the earth, comfort us when bad things happen to good people. We need the faith of Job to overcome our doubts, and to learn to trust in your infinite mercy. Teach us to trust in you, O Lord. For we are not made of stone, just weak human flesh, easily bruised, easily discouraged. In Jesus' name we pray. Amen.

Chapter 16
Stones of Hopelessness

As the conversations with his friends continue, Job's endurance wanes. Full of pain at the loss of his children and his wealth, weakened by the boils that cover his body, Job calls out to God.

> "But as a mountain falls at last, and its rock is moved from its place / As waters wear away the stones / and floods wash away the soil of the land / so you destroy the hope of man."
>
> **Job 14:18, 19**

Who could blame Job for his despair? How many of us could survive the deaths of our entire family, in addition to the loss of all our possessions? Then suffer through an attack of painful boils [think shingles], all within a short time span? How many of us would perish in our grief? How many lose faith in a loving, caring Abba? We are all only human after all. It does not take much to destroy our inner security.

Do you ever feel as if God is not listening to your prayers, or worse, that he does not care about us or our problems? Sometimes, in moments of extreme stress, it may feel as if God opens his hand and just lets us drop, screaming, through space. Our hearts constrict with fear and hopelessness. Sometimes we feel so numb, so locked into terror, we cannot even pray.

God! Where are you? Help me!

Just as Satan tempted Job, so Satan relentlessly tries to convince us that our heavenly Father does not care about us. In times of trouble, God alone has the answers. He is our hope, our comfort. Often when our lives go terribly wrong, our faith may be all we have. Remember the old saying that when you reach the end of your rope, just tie a knot and hang on! If we cling to hope, God will rescue us.

Pray that, like Job, we will be granted the strength to endure our trials, and triumph in the end.

O God, Father of love, comfort us in our trials. When we falter and stumble, when life seems too much to endure, strengthen us. We have only you, O Lord, to help us overcome our grief and pain. Grant us hope to carry on. In Jesus' name we pray. Amen.

Chapter 17
The Leviathan Heart of Stone

Toward the end of the Book of Job, this holy man grows bold and demands answers for his pain from God. The Lord's reply teaches Job, and us, our place in the heavenly scheme of things.

> **The LORD then said to Job: / Will we have arguing with the / Almighty by the critic? / Let him who would correct God give answer!**
>
> ### Job 40:1, 2

Job, of course, gave a meek answer to the Lord, and covered his mouth. God went on to address Job out of a storm. God compares the relative strength of his creatures: the power of a Behemoth (hippopotamus) and a Leviathan (crocodile) versus that of man. This long description of the animals' strength compared to that of a mere human being serves to put our relationship with the Almighty into perspective.

"His heart is hard as stone: / his flesh, as the lower millstone. / When he rises up, the mighty are afraid; / the waves of the sea fall back."

Job 41:15–17

Chastised by the Lord and understanding at last that God answers to no mere human for his deeds, Job repented in dust and ashes. To reward him for his steadfast faith, the Lord blessed the latter days of Job more than the earlier ones (Jb 42:12). This holy man prospered and lived one hundred and forty years, long enough to see his great-grandchildren. Then Job died, old and full of years (Jb 42:17).

What are we to glean from the long, and sometimes depressing, Book of Job? Is it that God only tests those whom he loves? A daunting thought! Why struggle to keep our faith, to do good works, if God sees our successes as an excuse to strike us down with calamities? There is a popular assumption that we can "earn" heaven by doing good works. Not so. Salvation is God's gift, a gift that cannot be earned by anything we do. Our good works should flow from our gratitude for the gifts, a sign of our acceptance of God's will in our lives.

Surely Abba does not punish us for living a good life. He may allow the devil to test us if we grow complacent. But God loves us. He never gives up on

51

us. Even if we argue with God, fall into despair and believe he has forgotten us, our heavenly Father still stands by us. Some believe that God weeps with us as we struggle with overwhelming grief. A comforting thought. Pray that the sin of complete despair never turns us away from the love and support waiting for us in God's arms.

Almighty Father, God of all, teach us to rely on you. We are your weak human creatures. Strengthen us, O Lord, when we fall into doubt about your love for us. For you alone are our rock, our strength, our salvation. In Jesus' name we pray. Amen.

Chapter 18
Scatter/Gather Stones

The book of Ecclesiastes in the Old Testament is concerned with the purpose and value of human life. The beginning verse is often quoted.

Vanity of vanities! All things are vanity!
Ecclesiastes 1:2

This beautiful poetic book reflects on the existence of a divine plan, hidden from humans. Life is considered an enigma, beyond human ability to solve. The often quoted third verse is familiar to most people. Only a few verses are quoted here.

There is an appointed time for everything, /
and a time for every affair under the
heavens. / A time to be born, and a time to
die...A time to weep, and a time to laugh; / a
time to mourn, and a time to dance. / A time
to scatter stones and a time to gather them.
Ecclesiastes 3:1, 2, 4, 5

What does it mean—a time to scatter stones and a time to gather them? Perhaps the verse is backward—a time to gather, then a time to scatter? Does it seem that we spend our entire lives gathering things we need? As infants we wail for food, consuming as much milk as needed to fill our empty stomachs. We cry for the comfort of dry clothing. We weep with loneliness, and are comforted by warm hugs. As toddlers we fight for toys, as many as we can gather and defend. As we grow older the toys grow more numerous and more costly. Housing, clothing, food, the security of being well loved—all meaningful things, gathered and defended. But when is the time to scatter? Jesus taught that we are blessed when we give to others, when we scatter our belongings. How many outfits can we wear at one time? That unused coat or extra blanket could be keeping a homeless person warm. The cost of a restaurant dinner could buy a week's groceries for a hungry family. A time to gather and a time to scatter.

But do the scatter/gather verses mean something else? What if a righteous person spends his or her entire life sharing possessions with the less fortunate? What if righteous people suffer a loss of fortune? The downward spiral toward poverty happens quickly—an overwhelming and expensive illness, the death of the principal wage earner, a natural disaster where home and possessions are swept away. Suddenly, people who had always been generous to the less fortunate find themselves on the receiving end of charity. A bitter blow to those who prided themselves on their independence! How galling to accept the help of others! It is more blessed to give than to be forced to receive! Yet God has a purpose for everything under the sun. Being needful teaches us to appreciate the concept of true charity. Refusing to accept help denies others their chance to be generous. Pray that we never fall into the trap of false pride or vanity.

O God, you who give us every good thing, teach us not only to share with others, but to accept help when it is offered. Banish false pride from our lives, O Lord. Bless us with hearts so open and generous, the angels will sing for joy. Nudge us with good intentions, O Lord of all. We need your guidance to gather and scatter according to your will. In Jesus' name we pray. Amen.

Chapter 19
Born Again Stones

As John the Baptist preached along the Jordan, people came to listen and be baptized. When certain leaders from the temple came forward to be saved, John proclaimed:

> **"...And do not presume to say to yourselves, 'We have Abraham as our father.' For I tell you, God can raise up children to Abraham from these very stones. Even now the ax lies at the root of the trees. Therefore every tree that does not bear good fruit will be cut down and thrown into the fire."**
> **Matthew 3:9, 10 and Luke 3:8**

John reprimands the leaders of the Jewish community (Pharisees and Sadducees) as they stepped forward to be baptized. Proud of their heritage as Sons of Abraham, these leaders may have submitted to the ceremony as a way of mocking John's message. Or in modern terms, they may have been hedging their bets, giving lip service to a popular prophet, just in case he did have some influence with God.

Going through religious rituals without a sincere heart did not fool John. It does not fool God, either. Faith without works is as dead as stones on the ground. God can raise up faith, even from stony hearts. But even Christians born to their faith must be fruitful with good works, showing their gratitude to God for the gift of faith. Does our faith resemble inert stones on the ground? Being baptized Christians does not guarantee our salvation! We need to express more than lip service to God's plan for our lives.

Have we been like the Pharisees? Do we go through the motions of piety as we attend church services, then roar out of the parking lot *(look out parishioners, this Christian wants to get home!)*? Does our weekend liturgy pass by without our pledging to put God first all week? Within our secret hearts, do we perform all religious requirements just for show? Or do we tithe, donate food and shelter to the poor, visit the sick, fast and pray? Do we share God's message of love with others, not only with our worldly goods, but with good example in our daily lives? We need to be more than stones on the ground, waiting for our Christian reward. Let us rise up as children of God and be born again into the true light of faith.

Pray that we may be fruitful with the gifts God has given us, so that we may rise from the stones of our apathy.

Heavenly Father, raise us up from our stony inertia. Teach us how to be fruitful in our service to you. Gift us with the courage and determination to share our faith with others. In Jesus' name we pray. Amen.

Chapter 20
Temptation Stones

Jesus was led into the desert by the Spirit to be tempted by the devil. He fasted forty days and forty nights and afterward was hungry. The tempter approached and said to [Jesus], "If you are the Son of God, command these stones to turn into bread." Jesus replied, "Scripture has it: / 'Not on bread alone is man to live / but on every utterance that comes from the mouth of God.'"

Matthew 4:1–4

After his cousin John baptized him, Jesus prepared for his ministry. He went into seclusion in the desert, praying and fasting for forty days and forty nights.

And he was hungry.

The Son of God lived in an earthly body, subject to human weaknesses. After a fast of forty days, Jesus' human body craved food. He must have been near fainting with hunger. Yet he had the strength of will to resist the devil's temptation to change stones into food.

Have you ever fasted, no food or water, for a day? Think of the weakness, the raging thirst and hunger, after just one day. Forty days of fasting sounds impossible for most of us. How could our soft human bodies survive? We might become weak enough to die! Yet Jesus did it, and survived the devil's temptation!

As often happens when we are weakened by life's difficult problems, the Tempter strikes with a seemingly harmless solution. Turn these stones to loaves of bread. Take the easy path—eat, drink and make merry, for tomorrow we die. How many times have we succumbed to temptations, minor and major? No one will care if we fail to support our parish. What will it matter if we do not fast this holy season? Who will notice if we skip the weekend services at our church?

Jesus' reply to Satan teaches us that our faith life should not be restricted to our bellies, or other earthly appetites, but the Word of God made flesh. We need to follow Jesus' example and resist the temptation to take the easy (if sinful) way out. Our parish desperately needs financial support. Fasting, not just from food or drink but from gossip and spite, will purify our bodies and hearts. Gathering as a community to give praise and thanksgiving to our Creator is one of the highest forms of worship.

Pray that Jesus will strengthen us when we feel tempted by the devil.

Heavenly Father, teach us to rely on you for our daily bread. Not only the bread that nourishes these frail earthly bodies, but the Bread of Life, which nourishes and sustains our spiritual lives. Your Son, Jesus, is our Bread and Drink. His body and blood fill us with every good thing. Let his every word strengthen our faith and sustain our spirits. In Jesus' name we pray. Amen.

Chapter 21
Pride Stones

> Next the devil took him to the holy city, set
> him on the parapet of the temple, and said,
> "If you are the Son of God, throw yourself
> down. Scripture has it: 'He will bid his
> angels take care of you; with their hands
> they will support you that you may never
> stumble on a stone.'"
> Jesus answered him, "Scripture also has
> it: / 'You shall not put the Lord your God
> to the test.'"
>
> **Matthew 4:5–7**

Matthew's gospel continues the account of Jesus'
temptation in the desert. The devil now asks our
Lord to display heavenly power. "Throw yourself
down" from the great height of the temple. "The
angels will catch you!" How well Satan knows our
human pride! Jesus, living in a human body, must
have felt tempted to give a little demonstration of his

Father's power. In older versions of the Bible, which use wonderfully poetic language, the devil says, "…the angels will bear you up, lest you dash your foot against a stone."(Ps 91:12)

Satan whispers a seductive message to Jesus, and to us. If we truly believe in God, we can throw ourselves into mortal and moral danger anytime, and God will protect and save our silly selves.

Jesus teaches that miracles are not to be demanded of God as evidence of his care for humankind. His answer gives us our guidelines. We shall not put our God to the test. In simpler terms, we are warned not to take dangerous risks with our lives, or our souls

"…lest you dash your foot against a stone."

The stones here are pride stones, the hard rocks of pride that block our path to the Father. Pride stones have as many faces as Mt. Rushmore. Pride makes us judge others for their sins. Pride keeps us home Sunday because we disagreed with a pastor's homily. Pride keeps us from reading Christian literature if it disagrees with our personal practices. Pride makes it difficult to forgive others who hurt us. Pride keeps us stiffnecked, nose in the air, until we stumble and fall into serious sin. Pride stones. Hard on the feet, hard on our souls.

Pray that God will strengthen us against the evil named pride.

Jesus, you met temptation and succeeded. Teach us to overcome our sinful pride. We need your help to avoid the pride stones of intolerance, old grudges, and anger. Just bearing your name as Christians is not enough to save us. Teach us humility as we place our trust in you. In your name we pray. Amen.

Chapter 22
Stumbling Stones

After John the Baptist was thrown into prison, he sent his disciples to ask of Jesus,

> **"Are you 'He who is to come' or are we to expect someone else?" Jesus replied, "Go and report to John what you have seen and heard. The blind recover their sight, cripples walk, lepers are cured, the deaf hear, dead men are raised to life, and the poor have the good news preached to them. Blest is that man who finds no stumbling [stone] block in me."**
>
> **Luke 7:18–23**

What is Jesus saying to the disciples of John, and also to people of our day? Jesus recounts the miraculous healings he performed in the Father's name: the blind see, the deaf hear, lepers are cured, dead men are raised to life, the poor have good news preached to them. Without bragging about his heavenly powers,

Jesus allows his followers to make their own decisions about his mission. Our Lord let his accomplishments speak for him.

How could they, and we, *not* believe in Jesus? What further proof did they need to truly believe that the Son of God loved them (and us) enough to walk this earth as healer and Savior?

Of course, hindsight is better sight. We believers, in today's world, know that Jesus was truly "He who is to come," the Messiah. Yet many of us still harbor doubts about the validity of Jesus and his earthly mission. Many people believe that Jesus was an ordinary man with extraordinary healing powers.

What do you believe?

Jesus said, **"Blest is that [person] who finds no stumbling [stone] in me."**

What private stumbling stones do we place in our path to faith? Is it so difficult to believe that God loves us, his lowly critters, enough to send his Son down to save us from our sins? God the Creator is all powerful, all loving, all merciful. Pray that we will put aside the stumbling stones of our personal doubt and accept Jesus as our Lord and Savior, he who has come!

Lord Jesus, help us to believe in you and your heavenly mission. We need the strength of your love and your wonderful power to banish all our doubts.

Help us to see clearly and to listen with open hearts to your message. Teach us to walk the narrow path of salvation. Just as you restored dead people to life, restore our dead and dying faith in you. We are poor sinners, O Lord. Help us to leap over the stumbling stones of our doubt with enlightened, faith-filled hearts. In your name we pray. Amen.

Chapter 23
Stone Water Jars

During the wedding at Cana,

At a certain point the wine ran out and Jesus' mother told him, "They have no more wine." Jesus replied, "Woman, how does this concern of yours involve me? My hour has not yet come." His mother instructed those waiting on table, "Do whatever he tells you." As prescribed for Jewish ceremonial washing, there were at hand six stone water jars, each one holding fifteen to twenty-five gallons. "Fill those with water," Jesus ordered, at which they filled them to the brim. "Now," he said, "draw some out and take it to the waiter in charge." They did as he instructed them. The waiter in charge tasted the water made wine [and later called it choice wine].

John 2:3–9

What does this scripture story say to us? The obvious and most popular meaning is that Mary intercedes for us with Jesus. She is our help for problems, even minor problems such as running out of party food and drink. At parties today, if the food and drink run low, the party ends and people head for home. But in Jesus' day, parties, especially lavish Jewish wedding celebrations, went on for days, maybe even a week or more. It was a serious breach of hospitality, a major embarrassment, for a groom to run out of wine or food before the prescribed party time ran its course. So Mary's concern for the hapless groom in this reading showed her wonderful compassion. It also reveals just how powerful is our heavenly mother's request for help. Even though her son turned her down at first, Jesus did work this water-into-wine miracle at his mother's request.

Notice the size of the stone water jars. A fifteen- to twenty-five gallon stone water jug is a big container. They were called ceremonial washing jars. Did the people immerse their bodies into the jars? Or did they dip out a prescribed amount of water and pour it over their hands, heads, and feet in a purifying ceremony? How did the waiters manage to pour out a sample of the water-made-wine into a glass for the chief wine steward to taste? A stone jar containing twenty-five gallons of water must have been heavy! How did these servants manage to lift the stone water jars and pour out the water-made-wine? Would the resulting rush of water drown anyone standing nearby? Maybe nothing is too big to hold a miracle, not even a huge stone water jar.

Are the concerns of present-day hosts or hostesses too insignificant for Jesus to help with? Mary's reply gives us the answer: **"Do whatever he tells you."** Pray that we, like Mary, will have the faith and confidence to seek Jesus' help with all our problems.

Jesus, our help and our salvation, teach us to turn to you with our problems, big and small. Mary, our heavenly mother, intercede for us with your beloved son. When troubles threaten to drown out our good intentions, pray that we will remember this scripture story of water changed into wine. Nothing is impossible with Jesus, our Lord and our God. Through him, with him, and in him we pray now and forever. Amen.

Chapter 24
Stones of Denial

Jesus said, "Ask and you will receive. Seek, and you will find. Knock, and it will be opened to you. For the one who asks, receives. The one who seeks, finds. The one who knocks, enters. Would one of you hand your son a stone when he asks for a loaf, or a poisonous snake when he asks for a fish? If you, with all your sins, know how to give your children what is good, how much more will your heavenly Father give good things to anyone who asks him!"

Matthew 7:7–10

During his lengthy sermon on the mount, Jesus instructs his disciples, and us, to trust in our heavenly Father. The stone here represents something cold and hard and inedible. What father could be so stonehearted as to give a rock to a child hungry for bread?

"You're hungry, kid? Here, eat a stone sandwich."

In today's world, a parent denying food to a truly hungry child could be arrested and charged with child abuse, or child neglect. Even homeless parents have programs to help feed their children, including food stamps, Special Supplemental Nutrition Program for Women, Infants, and Children (WIC), and food kitchens. A parent would be hard-hearted indeed to deny food or other necessities to helpless children.

So it is with our heavenly Father. He wants to feed us good things. We have only to ask and to trust in Abba's generosity. Do you think human parents love their children more than our heavenly Father loves each of us? Jesus gives us the answer.

> **"If you, with all your sins, know how to give your children what is good, how much more will your heavenly Father give good things to anyone who asks him!"**
>
> **Luke 11:13**

In this passage Jesus teaches us to pray to Abba, because God is a loving father. The message is clear. We are to depend on the loving kindness of our heavenly Father. We are to pray for all our needs, and trust that God will know what is best for us.

Sometimes what we pray for is not in our best interests. God may turn down requests for the good of our souls. Yet the Father always listens to our petitions.

He gave us the Bread of Life! What further proof do we need of his loving care?

Pray for the gift of trust in the Father's will for our lives.

Heavenly Father, feed us with the Bread of Life. Like helpless children, we rely on you for all our needs. We need your love and direction in our lives. Teach us to rely on your loving kindness. We pray this through your son our Lord, Jesus Christ. Amen.

Chapter 25
Millstones

In the midst of a sermon that touched on ambition and envy, the disciples ask Jesus: "Who is of the greatest importance in the kingdom of heaven?" Jesus' reply is not what they expect. He calls over a little child and urges the disciples to become like innocent children.

> Jesus said, "But it would be better if anyone who leads astray one of these simple believers were to be plunged into the sea with a great millstone fastened around his neck."
>
> **Mark 9:42**

In Matthew's version, Jesus said,

> Whoever welcomes one such child for my sake welcomes me. On the other hand, if anyone would lead astray one of these little ones who believe in me, it would be better

for such persons if a millstone would be tied
around their neck and they would be flung
into the depths of the sea to drown.
(paraphrased)

See Matthew 18:5–7

A millstone was a great wheel of stone used to grind
grain, usually placed in a stream to take advantage of
the water's power. The stone here is meant to be a
dead weight, a punishing stone, a weapon of destruc-
tion to drag down sinners who lead others astray.

In Jesus' day, a millstone as a method of punishment may have been used for serious sinners. A millstone around the neck could also mean being
weighted down by sin, especially the sins of scandal
(bad example, deliberate leading of innocent souls
into sin, the corruption of innocence). Jesus' sermon
stresses that innocence must be protected.

What are the millstones in our sinful lives? Have we
been vigilant in protecting the innocence of the young?
Do we fight in the very real battle against child pornog-
raphy? Have we picketed nude bars? Protested to our
congressmen about filthy programs on television and
the Internet? Have we worked hard to prevent the millstones of evil example? God judges not only the sins we
avoid, but how we protest the public evil of others.

What other sins drag us down? God made our spirits and souls to rise to him. When we are dragged

down by inertia or our sinful human nature, the heavy weight of our sins separates us from his loving presence. Pray that our loving Father will remove the millstones around our necks before we drown in our own sinfulness.

Heavenly Father, save us from the weight of our sins. Lighten our loads. Remove the sinful millstones that drag us down, away from the light of your love. Remind us to always work to protect the innocence of those in our care. In Jesus' name we pray. Amen.

Chapter 26
Judgment Stones

During the Feast of the Dedication in Jerusalem, Jesus was teaching some Jews in the temple who had gathered around him, and said,

> "The Father and I are one." When some of the Jews again reached for rocks to stone him, Jesus protested to them, "Many good deeds have I shown you from the Father. For which of these do you stone me?" "It is not for any "good deed" that we are stoning you," the Jews retorted, "but for blaspheming. You who are only a man are making yourself God."
> John 10:30–33

What is the gospel writer telling us in this confrontation between Jesus and his enemies? Remember, many enemies of Jesus had witnessed miracles, healings, even dead people brought back to life. How could they *not* believe that Jesus is God's Son? Perhaps the

Jews mentioned in this story had not really seen Jesus at work. Mass communication was not available then— no television, no radio news programs, no Internet. Jesus had just the tiny network of believers who spread the Good News, and there was a large group of disbelievers who spread false rumors about him.

What would your reaction be if you watched the six o'clock news this evening and a man or woman claimed to be God's only child? Would you snort in disbelief and vote with the remote? The Jewish people in this reading voted with what was available to them at that time, the stones of judgment. They **"...again reached for rocks to stone him."** Because ..."**You... are only a man...making yourself God."**

What is the lesson we take from this scene? Are we to judge others by their words, or by their deeds? What if the words are so outrageous, so foreign to our nature or faith, we must turn away in confusion? Many of Jesus' words are hard for believers to take, and even more difficult to live by. Yet, as God's Son, only Jesus has the words of everlasting life.

But what about the deeds? Even though Jesus performed miracles, healings, and even raised people from the dead, still people cast stones of judgment at him.

Have we ever cast stones about people who seem too good to be true? When Mother Teresa died, some said she should have used her power to help the poor in the world by promoting family planning. Casting stones at a modern-day saint!

Do we feel threatened by the good deeds of holy people? What does that say about our values, our belief in Jesus' words? Pray that the Spirit of God will guide our actions in these confusing days.

Spirit of God, blow through our lives, cluttered with disbelief, envy, and false judgment of our neighbors. Teach us to rely on Jesus' words, the words of everlasting life. Help us not to throw stones of judgment against others, especially at those people who seem "too good to be true." In Jesus' name we pray. Amen.

Chapter 27
Vanity Stones

After Jesus finished his long teachings in the temple, his disciples marveled over the buildings in the temple area.

> **Jesus said, "Do you see all these buildings? I assure you, not one stone will be left on another—it will all be torn down."**
> **Matthew 24:3**

Jesus' message points out the foibles of ancient and modern vanity. Even the grandest of humankind's buildings and creations are merely temporary. The stones here are building blocks, huge rocks hewn from a quarry by slave labor. It must have taken years of hard labor (forty years, according to the chief priest who condemned Jesus) to build the temple. Yet Jesus is predicting it will be torn down until not one stone rests on another.

This must have been a shocking revelation to the haughty people of Jesus' day. They were proud of their temple—the huge, gleaming building adorned with jewels and precious stones, the house of God, and the center of their worship events. Yet this poor teacher, Jesus of Nazareth, predicts to his ragtag followers that the temple will be torn down. No wonder the Sanhedrin charged him with blasphemy!

Today people build memorials and huge expensive buildings of worship. Does our Creator look more kindly on these houses of stone and those who labor to build them? God, the all powerful Creator of heaven and earth, deserves large, beautiful houses built in his honor, but does he prefer them? Who can know the mind of God? Even the most expensive building is temporary, subject to the wear and tear of time. Lavish buildings may be vanities, showcases of people with a misguided sense of values. Does it make sense to divert riches to the construction of beautiful stone buildings when there are starving people among us? Maybe Jesus wants us to build up a sound spiritual and prayer life instead? Our Savior told us to feed the hungry, clothe the naked, give shelter to the homeless. Perhaps we could volunteer time and talent to building homes for Habitat? Jesus never encouraged us to build stone temples as a way of giving honor to God. Our Creator does not need the vanity of beautiful stone buildings to know that we love and honor him.

Pray that we will not succumb to the pervasive sin of vanity.

O Lord, teach us a good sense of values. Where there is hunger, teach us to share. When homeless people appeal to us, nudge us to provide them shelter. Inspire us to clothe the naked, the poor people who shiver in the cold without adequate clothing. Make us generous O Lord, to those who need help. Teach us to find beauty in sunsets, the birds of the fields, and the faces of strangers. For you are our Creator God, the Master Builder. You have no need for humans to build you a beautiful house. As always, we make this prayer in Jesus' name. Amen.

Chapter 28
Weapon Stones

After Jesus calmed the storm on the lake (**"Who can this be that even the wind and the sea obey him?"**):

> They came to Gerasene territory on the other side of the lake. As [Jesus] got out of the boat, he was immediately met by a man from the tombs who had an unclean spirit. The man had taken refuge among the tombs; he could no longer be restrained even with a chain. In fact, he had frequently been secured with handcuffs and chains, but had pulled the chains apart and smashed the fetters. No one had proved strong enough to tame him. Uninterruptedly night and day, amid the tombs and on the hillsides, he screamed and gashed himself with stones.
>
> **Mark 5:1–5**

How frightened those early followers of Jesus must have felt as they watched the man who was demented by many unclean spirits, a man notorious for his wild deeds. Their fear intensified as the man ran up to Jesus and did him homage, shrieking in a loud voice. The gospel story does not mention whether the disciples ran away or stayed to protect their Master. In any event, Jesus called the unclean spirits out of the suffering man and cast them into a herd of swine. The herd of about two thousand swine then plunged into the sea and drowned.

The possessed man had tried to force the demons out of his body by gashing himself with stones. Yet even that drastic measure did not bring him relief. It took Jesus' power and compassion to heal the suffering man. Stones in this story are self-inflicting weapons.

Today's evil spirits might be drugs, alcohol, prejudice, self-hatred, gluttony, or sexual excesses. No matter how hard we try to gouge our weaknesses out of our body, it takes God's power to heal us. Perhaps this explains the success of programs such as Alcoholics Anonymous, and other drug-dependency programs. These self-help programs focus on giving up personal power and turning addictions over to a higher power.

So what are the unclean spirits in our lives today? What demons torment our lives? What weapon stones do we use, instead of turning our lives over to God for healing? Do we fast and exercise when trying to control gluttony? Have we tried to quit drinking, or taking drugs, cold turkey? Do we try to avoid people of other races and colors? How successful are we in controlling our demons without God's help? Only our Lord has the power to cast out the personal evil that destroys our lives. We must turn our addictions over to him, or risk abject failure.

Pray that the God of mercy and power will cast out our personal demons, the unclean spirits that keep us in chains.

God of mercy, help us today. Teach us to recognize what keeps us chained away from your forgiveness. Heal us of our addictions. Help us to turn to you for help instead of relying on our weak and useless weapon stones. In Jesus's name we pray. Amen.

Chapter 29
Singing Stones

After the disciples put Jesus on the colt and led him toward Jerusalem, they began to rejoice and praise God loudly.

> **"Blessed is he who comes as king / in the name of the Lord! / Peace in heaven / and glory in the highest!"**
> **Some of the Pharisees in the crowd said to [Jesus], "Teacher, rebuke your disciples."**
> **[Jesus] replied, "If they were to keep silent, I tell you the very stones would cry out."**
>
> **Luke 19:39, 40**

What an astonishing story! Can you imagine the shock waves that would ripple through that jubilant crowd if the very stones of the field would start to sing the praises of Jesus? Perhaps the roadway into Jerusalem was paved with cobblestones. Early writings do not give us much detail. We know that

Jerusalem stood on a hill and the road into the city went uphill and through the gates. Some of Jesus's followers took off their cloaks and placed them on the roadway for the colt to walk across. Perhaps the paving stones were slippery. In any event, when told to quiet his disciples, Jesus' answer to his enemies created a wonderful scenario.

"I tell you the very stones would cry out."

The stones here represent inanimate objects (dead things) that could, if summoned, spring to life as Jesus rides by.

Are we like paving stones—dead things to be walked on by the enemies of Christ? Do we keep a stony silence as friends, relatives, or co-workers deny the living presence of God in our lives? Keeping silent when others are vilifying God speaks volumes about our faith life. Are we afraid to lift our voices to defend our faith for fear others will think we are religious fanatics? Better to be thought a religious nut than to act as if we are indifferent to our God!

Are we afraid to sing praise to God? Does the joyful singing in church find us mute and unresponsive? Who cares if our voices are not perfect? God only demands a willing spirit, not a professional singing voice. Let us open our mouths and cry out with joy as our Lord and Master passes by! Pray that Jesus will turn us into singing stones.

O Lord, teach us to lift our hearts and voices in praise of you. You are our Savior, our Redeemer, the One who died for our sins. Help us overcome the stony hearts that keep us mute and unresponsive to your love. You have done so much for us. The least we can do is sing your praises! In Jesus' name we pray. Amen.

Chapter 30
Building Stones

As Jesus approaches Jerusalem, riding on the donkey, he weeps over the sinful city.

> **"Days will come upon you when your enemies encircle you with a rampart, hem you in, and press you hard from every side. They will wipe you out, you and your children within your walls, and leave not a stone on a stone within you, because you failed to recognize the time of your visitation."**
>
> **Luke 19:43, 44**

This is a tough-love warning from Jesus. His prediction of the fall of Jerusalem became reality within a few years after his death. Jerusalem, the holy city of the Chosen People, fell to its enemies. The Temple was leveled. No stone was left upon a stone. All because the people of Jesus' day did not accept him as the Messiah.

Yet if Jerusalem had not been destroyed and the Chosen People scattered to the ends of the earth, the spread of Christianity might have been delayed. The Jewish people were defeated, deported to foreign lands, enslaved by their captors. Discouraged and overwhelmed by these burdens, many captives turned to the New Way, the newly-formed Christian faith, for meaning and comfort.

What will it take to turn our sinful selves toward God? If we fail to recognize Jesus in our cities (our lives), will our lives crumble before the power of the Lord? Jesus wept over Jerusalem because of its sin. Does he weep over our sins too? Have we turned our back on our Redeemer? Do we fail to recognize Jesus and his path for holy living in our daily lives? It is so easy to become caught up in daily routine, work, family, entertainment. Remember that Jesus died for us. What have we done for him today?

God is a God of love, ready to forgive, ready to welcome us back into the warmth of his kingdom, to lead us to the New Way of Jesus Christ.

Pray now that we will accept and welcome Jesus, whether he comes as a humble carpenter riding on a lowly beast of burden, or on a cloud with the power and might of all heaven behind him. Let us welcome him!

O Lord, you are the living stone come down from heaven. Teach us to build our faith life on you. We want to be cities of stone for you. Strengthen our faith life. Help us to be unconquered rocks of faith, in your name. Amen.

Chapter 31
Cornerstone/Keystone

After Jesus' triumphant entry into Jerusalem, he drove the buyers and sellers out of the temple. He then gave many teachings, using parables. After the parable about the vineyard tenants who killed the master's slaves and eventually the son, he said:

> **"Did you never read in the scriptures, /
> 'The stone which the builders rejected / has
> become the keystone [cornerstone] of the
> structure. / It was the Lord who did this
> and we find it marvelous to behold.'?"**
>
> **Matthew 21:42**

Jesus quoted Isaiah's Stone of Zion verse. This verse represents God's covenant with the house of David and his descendants:

> **Therefore, thus says the Lord GOD: See, I
> am laying a stone in Zion,…A precious**

cornerstone as a sure foundation: / he who
puts his faith in it shall not be shaken.
Isaiah 28:16

The ancient prophet, Isaiah, foretold Jesus, the
Messiah, would be the cornerstone of faith. Isaiah's
teachings were ignored by the people of his day. The
Messiah would also be rejected by the house of
Israel. Yet this cornerstone lives on as the keystone of
our faith. Jesus continued:

"For this reason, I tell you, the kingdom of
God will be taken away from you and given
to a nation that will yield a rich harvest.
[The man who falls upon that stone will be
smashed to bits; and he on whom it falls
will be crushed.]"
Matthew 21:43, 44

Jesus is the stone rejected who became the cornerstone of our faith. The descendants of David rejected
him, so he built up a new church containing believers
of other nations (Gentiles, or non-Jews). The stone
that falls and crushes the unbelievers is the judgment
stone. The stone (Jesus) can be either a salvation
stone or a judgment stone. It is up to us to either
believe or reject him.

What is the cornerstone of our individual faith? Do
we believe in the Old Testament law, an eye for an

eye, the harsh judgment of sinners? Do we base our actions on the popular culture today, which allows human lives to be snuffed out by abortion, euthanasia, and capital punishment? Or is our faith based on Jesus' teachings to love one another, forgive enemies, turn the other cheek? If we wear the name of Jesus Christ as Christians, should we not live out his teachings? Pray that the keystone of our faith strengthens us to live according to his gospel teachings.

O Jesus, teach us to be like you, kind and forgiving to those who hurt us. Bless us every day as we struggle to build a better world through our faith. Inspire us to build on heavenly values, not on the worldly ways of revenge and hate. In your name, O Lord, forever and ever. Amen.

Chapter 32
Pretty Stones

As Jesus was teaching in the temple:

While some people were speaking about how the temple was adorned with costly stones and votive offerings, Jesus said, "All that you see here—the days will come when there will not be left a stone upon another stone that will not be thrown down."

Luke 21:5, 6

The stones here were expensive bits of stone, gemstones, rubies, lapis lazuli, and perhaps diamonds and pearls. All beautiful stones shined up and put on display. The disciples, most of them poor fishermen, marveled over the outward beauty (and expense) of the temple.

The temple in Jerusalem must have been beautiful, and awe-inspiring—an ancient tribute to the God of the Jewish covenant. Its inner altars of sacrifice were lined with gold. Read 1 Kings, Chapter 6, for a detailed description. Adorned with precious stones, the huge building took forty years to build. No wonder the followers of Jesus reacted with wonder. A modern-day comparison might be the awe and wonder people experience when visiting St. Peter's in Rome.

What are the pretty stones that overwhelm us today? Do beautiful buildings cause us to stop and stare in wonder? Or are we so jaded by human-made wonders that we glance away without really seeing or appreciating the years of labor and inspiration needed to create the buildings?

What about God-made beauty? Sunrise or sunset, available every day for our appreciation. Fresh snow clinging to pine boughs, and air so crisp it stirs our heart to gratitude for the warmth of an evening's fire. An infant's smile, beautiful enough to bring tears to the most stiff-necked adult. The sight of a black, snowcapped mountain rising from the desert floor. The majesty of the Grand Canyon at sunset, shimmering crimson and gold, is awe-inspiring enough to bring gasps, even from weary tourists. But sometimes we become so caught up in the wonder of earthly beauty, we forget the origin of all beauty. These natural wonders were created by our all powerful God. Do we worship beauty or the One who created all beauty?

Jesus warned that beautiful buildings adorned with pretty stones will eventually be torn down and return to dust. His message to his followers reminds us that earthy beauty is temporary. We are warned not to put our faith in bits of colored rock, but on the true rock of life: Jesus. We are not to covet goods, no matter how beautiful, but to look higher, to God. Pray that our faith will not be dazzled by earthly beauty, but grounded in our true treasure, Jesus our Savior.

Creator God, teach us to place our faith in you. You do not need earthly buildings to give honor to your name. All beauty, all precious stones, all treasures belong to you, who created all things. Gift us with discernment to know what is truly good for us. In Jesus' name we pray. Amen.

Chapter 33
Punishing Stones

After praying in the Garden of Olives, Jesus reappeared in the temple area, sat down and began to teach the people.

> The scribes and the Pharisees led a woman forward who had been caught in adultery. They made her stand there in front of everyone. "Teacher," they said to [Jesus], "this woman has been caught in the act of adultery. In the law, Moses ordered such women to be stoned. What have you to say about this case?" (They posed this question to trap him, so that they could have something to accuse him of.) Jesus bent down and started tracing on the ground with his finger. When they persisted in their questioning, he straightened up and said to them, "Let the man among you who has no sin be the first to cast a stone at her." A

second time he bent down and wrote on the ground.

John 8:3–8

John is the only gospel writer to mention the woman caught in adultery. The punishment for adultery in those days was death by stoning. Where is the man caught in adultery with this woman? John does not mention him. Perhaps in those days, when men were masters of the house and women were possessions of their husbands, the adulterous man did not receive any punishment.

In any event, here is a woman caught in serious sin, brought before the Master who taught love and forgiveness. She must have expected a horrible, public punishment for her sins. Instead, Jesus not only forgave her, he refused to even accuse her!

A silent movie, "The King of Kings," shows this scene in stark black and white. There was no spoken dialogue, just background music and subtitles along the bottom of the giant screen. During this scene, as men stand nearby with stones ready to fling at her, Jesus draws in the dust at the feet of the accused woman. Each man reads a different judgment written in the dust, according to his sins.

Murderer. Thief. Liar.

One by one, as the men read the dusty written words, they drop their stones. An impressive sound, perhaps on a base drum, bongs as each rock drops to the ground.

Lesson: Jesus will judge each of us. It is not our job to cast stones at others. Only Jesus knows the hearts of sinners. Pray that we will learn to let go of our judgment stones, before we are judged and found wanting!

Jesus, all powerful judge, all forgiving Savior, forgive us for the times we clung to our judgment stones against those who hurt us. Teach us how to drop our weapons against others. For only you have the power, and the mercy, to judge the weaknesses and the sins of all of us. In your name we pray. Amen.

Chapter 34
Stones of Darkness

Jesus, called to the home of his friends Martha, Mary, and Lazarus, is saddened to hear that Lazarus had died four days before. Yet Martha believes that Jesus can bring her brother back to life. They approach the tomb.

> Once again troubled in spirit, Jesus approached the tomb. It was a cave with a stone laid across it. "Take away the stone," Jesus directed. Martha, the dead man's sister, said to him, "Lord, it has been four days now; surely there will be a stench!" Jesus replied, "Did I not assure you that if you believed, you would see the glory of God displayed?" They then took away the stone....[Jesus] called loudly, "Lazarus, come out!" The dead man came out, bound hand and foot with linen strips, his face

wrapped in a cloth. "Untie him," Jesus told them, "and let him go free."
John 11:38–41, 43, 44

What a fantastic scene! A man, four days in the tomb, comes forth at Jesus' command. In the days before chemical embalming, dead people were placed in the tomb before sundown on the day they died. Their bodies were rubbed with ritual spices and wrapped in linen. In the hot climate of Israel, it did not take long for corruption to invade a corpse. The stone across the tomb entrance kept odors at bay as the body returned to dust. Yet Jesus said, **"Take away the stone."**

The stone here represents whatever blocks us from the light of God's love.

No matter how dead in sin we are, how odorous our sins, Jesus wants to roll away the stone that keeps us imprisoned in darkness.

"Come out!"

But, like Martha, we sometimes protest. Embarrassed about the stench of our sins, we cling to the darkness. We hide behind stones of shame, afraid to accept the light of God's forgiving love. Like guilty children deep in a cave, we are afraid our heavenly Father will not forgive us. Jesus calls us to come out of our hiding places.

When his Master called, Lazarus did not protest. He did not show fear or shame.

The dead man came out, bound hand and foot with linen strips, his face wrapped in a cloth.

Why do we protest? Why allow anything to keep us from the light of Jesus' love? Or are we like the newly risen Lazarus, still tied hand and foot by sin and guilt?

"Untie him and let him go free."

Jesus calls us out of our own personal darkness. It is up to us to answer his call to the light. Pray that we will accept his call when Jesus rolls back our stones of darkness.

Jesus, healer, forgiver of all our sins, teach us to accept your saving light. Heal us of all darkness that keeps us away from you. Encourage us when we feel deadened, defeated by the forces of darkness, buried in sin. In your name we pray for hope and healing. Amen.

Chapter 35
A Stone's Throw

At the Mount of Olives, the night before his death, Jesus

> **...withdrew from them about a stone's throw, then went down on his knees and prayed.**
>
> **Luke 22:41**

How far is a stone's throw? It depends upon the strength of your throwing arm. For the sports-minded, a good throw may mean from the outfield to home plate, or from the thirty-yard line through the goal posts. But for most people today, a stone's throw is merely a metaphor for a short distance.

In Jesus' time, a stone's throw meant a definite distance away, perhaps one hundred feet. Far enough away for privacy, yet close enough to call for help. Jesus wanted to pray to the Father for strength. He needed privacy for his prayer. Jesus knew the horrible fate approaching—death on the cross. Perhaps he wished to spare his followers the sight of his anguish.

Luke goes on to describe Jesus' agony in the garden:

> **An angel then appeared to [Jesus] from heaven to strengthen him. In his anguish he prayed with all the greater intensity, and his sweat became like drops of blood falling to the ground.**
>
> ### Luke 22:43, 44

What agony our Savior suffered in the garden of prayer! Because he was human, he would suffer the full physical torture of crucifixion, and his divine nature anticipated the terrible pain. Jesus knew that not only would he die a horrible death, but his friends would abandon him during his hours of need. No wonder Jesus' sweat became like drops of blood and the Father sent an angel to strengthen him.

Meanwhile, just a stone's throw from Jesus' agony in the garden, his friends slept. Could *we* have stayed awake to pray with the Master? Or would our human nature have taken over? Do we distance ourselves from the problems and agonies of others? Have we tried to keep a stone's throw from our friends when a crisis overwhelms them? If someone is in real trouble, even dying, do we visit them, or keep a safe distance, just in case their problems are "catching"? Do we sleep while others weep?

What about when a real crisis hits your family?

When trouble comes, sometimes you have to withdraw from your friends and seek help from a higher power, the Father. The stone's throw is a measuring device. What measure do we use to separate ourselves from earthly concerns and seek the Father's help? Pray that the Father will send us help when we are in desperate need.

Heavenly Father, you sent an angel to your son to comfort him in the Garden of Gethsemane. Help us when we are in desperate trouble. Send your comforting angel, and faithful friends, to strengthen us. In Jesus' name we pray, now and at the hour of our death. Amen.

Chapter 36
Stones of Despair

After Jesus died on the cross, a friend, Joseph of Arimathea, claimed his body for burial.

> **When evening fell, a wealthy man from Arimathea arrived, Joseph by name. He was another of Jesus's disciples, and had gone to request the body of Jesus. Thereupon Pilate issued an order for its release. Taking the body, Joseph wrapped it in fresh linen and laid it in his own new tomb which had been hewn from a formation of rock. Then he rolled a huge stone across the entrance of the tomb and went away.**
>
> **Matthew 27:57–60**

Joseph of Arimathea, a member of the Sanhedrin, kept his allegiance to Jesus a secret. Yet when our Savior died, Joseph stepped forward to offer his own tomb for a burial place for Jesus. It must have taken great courage, in the shadow of the cross, to go to the ruler, Pilate, and ask for the body. Usually cruci-fied victims stayed on their crosses until the bodies rotted, as a Roman gesture of power. Not only did Joseph risk the censure of temple priests and scribes, he put his own life on the line to defy Roman rule. Yet Pilate released the body, and Joseph's courage and generosity is still remembered today.

Rolling the huge stone across the tomb was an act of finality to the followers of Jesus. *Our friend is dead, they thought. He who claimed to be God's son died a shameful death. Now he is buried. Roll the stone across. Let us turn our backs, walk away, and forget we ever knew him.*

What despair these first believers must have felt! All their plans, their hopes, their dreams, shut away now, sealed off behind the tombstone. The disciples had given up home, family and livelihood to follow Jesus. Now it was over. Jesus, their teacher, mentor, Messiah, was dead. They thought it was the end. It was only the beginning.

What are the tombstones in our lives? What shuts out Jesus' light and his message of eternal life? What blocks our view of the Savior? What circumstances have caused us to shut away our faith? What stones of despair make us turn our backs and walk away from God's loving care?

Sometimes the death of a loved one triggers a long period of anger against God. Overwhelming grief is a test of our faith life. Prolonged anger against our Creator only hurts us. Despair seals us away from the warmth and love of our heavenly Father.

Jesus waited in the tomb for three days before rising to light and love. How long will we wait before we return to our loving Father? God waits for us now. Pray that Jesus will help us roll back the stone.

Loving Father, teach us to trust in your goodness and mercy. Grant us the courage of Joseph of Arimathea to step forward when friends need our support. Help us roll back the stones of despair that keep us from you. In Jesus' name we pray. Amen.

Chapter 37
Seal the Stone

> The next day [following the crucifixion]...the chief priests and the Pharisees called at Pilate's residence. "Sir," they said, "we have recalled that the impostor...made the claim, 'After three days I will rise.' You should issue an order having the tomb kept under surveillance until the third day. Otherwise his disciples may go and steal him and tell the people, 'He has been raised from the dead!' This final imposture would be worse than the first." Pilate told them, "You have a guard. Go and secure the tomb as best you can." So they went and kept it under surveillance of the guard, after fixing a seal to the stone.
>
> Matthew 27:62–66

Even after killing Jesus, his enemies were afraid of him. They sought to "seal him in death," by placing a seal on the stone. The authorities were afraid that

Jesus's disciples would steal his body and claim that Jesus rose from the dead. As if a seal around a stone would keep the Son of God from rising from the dead!

The enemies of Jesus hoped to keep the body of the crucified troublemaker sealed away. Were they ashamed of their deeds: the mock trial, the scourging, the hanging on the cross of a sinless man? Did they want to forget their guilt by hiding the body behind a sealed stone?

What do we try to hide behind our stones of guilt? Have we "crucified" another's reputation by gossip and scandal? What misdeeds have we buried in our lives behind the smooth stones of respectability? Are we so ashamed of our sins that we refuse to confess them? Jesus reassured us that no sin is so great that our loving Father will not forgive us. Let us resolve now to roll back our stones of fear and guilt and accept the gift of forgiveness.

Another stone in our lives may be the one we hide behind whenever someone questions our faith. Religious faith is such a personal thing. Sometimes it is difficult to discuss it with people of other religions. Are we afraid their probing questions will destroy our faith? Or are we on shaky ground when Bible verses are quoted to us? Just what do we believe about God, Jesus, the Holy Spirit, the concept of the Eucharist? Honest discussion about religion should not hurt our faith, but strengthen it.

Have we tried to seal away doubts about our faith by hiding them behind barriers of secrecy and fear? Maybe it is time to make a retreat, join a scripture study program, or become active in the RCIA. Other Christians share the same questions and doubts. Perhaps it is time to escape from behind that big stone sealed across our faith life.

Pray that Jesus will roll back our stones and open us to light and life in God's kingdom.

O Jesus, you died for our sins. Help us to roll back our stones of doubt and guilt. Open our hearts to your loving example. Teach us to trust in the Father's forgiving love. In Jesus' name we pray. Amen.

Chapter 38
Unseal the Stone

> **After the sabbath, as the first day of the week was dawning, Mary Magdalene came with the other Mary to inspect the tomb. Suddenly there was a mighty earthquake, as the angel of the Lord descended from heaven. He came to the stone, rolled it back, and sat on it.**
>
> **Matthew 28:1–2**

What powerful images: an earthquake, and the angel of the Lord descending from heaven. How the women must have marveled to see the huge stone rolled back. So much for the schemes of the Pharisees and the chief priests. Not even a huge stone, sealed and guarded by soldiers, could block Jesus from the light of day or block our Savior from rising again! Don't you love the image of the angel rolling back the stone and sitting on it? Such disdain for mere human schemes. Seal the stone, indeed!

What would it take to unseal and roll back the stones of our unbelief? What kind of upheaval in our personal lives would it take to turn our lives around? God does not often send down an angel to dramatize his power. Yet we need to search for the hand of God in ordinary events. The unexpected baby who brings great joy to reluctant parents. A job lost, then replaced by a better opportunity. An alcoholic loved one who joins AA. All these things are God-prompted.

Sometimes we humans take credit for God's intervention in our lives. We pray so diligently for help when something in our life goes wrong. Yet when relief comes, we forget to say thank you to the One responsible. We may think we finally solved our problem and mop our brow with relief. Or we give credit to a friend, or relative, who may have helped us out. Yet it was usually God who sent other people to help us. The angels have enough to do, ordinary people serve as messengers here on earth. We always thank our friends for helping us. Do we remember to thank God for the blessing of loving friends?

God hears our prayers. He always answers, even though sometimes the answer is so slow in coming that we forget what we prayed for. Sometimes God's answer is no because our heavenly Father has an alternate, and better, plan for our lives. But all too often, even when we receive what we pray for, we fail to acknowledge it, or thank our Creator for his blessings.

Pray that we will not need an angel and an earthquake to roll back our stones of ingratitude.

God of power and great saving love, teach us how to roll back the stones that keep us from your light. Jesus, your Son, waited three days in the tomb. Gift us with patience as we await your saving angel. Let not our human mistrust and pride keep us from appreciating your loving care. Roll back our stones of disbelief and ingratitude, O Lord. We need to see your light! In Jesus' name we pray. Amen.

Chapter 39
The Stoning of Stephen

After the death and resurrection of Jesus, the number of disciples grew so numerous that the original apostles were swamped with duties. Unable to keep up with daily responsibilities, the Twelve directed the assembly to appoint other men to help. One man so assigned was Stephen, a man filled with grace and power, who worked great wonders and signs among the people. Jealous members of the Sanhedrin, unable to beat him during debates, brought charges of blasphemy against Stephen. This first martyr stood before the Sanhedrin, the ruling body of the temple in Jerusalem. He gave a long discourse describing the Jewish history beginning with Abraham, proving that Jesus was truly the Christ, the promised Messiah. The members of the Sanhedrin listened intently to Stephen until the young man said,

"You stiff-necked people...you are always opposing the Holy Spirit just as your

fathers did before you...You...have
become...betrayers and murderers. You who
received the law through the ministry of
angels have not observed it." Those who
listened to his words were stung to the
heart.

Acts 7:51–54

Stephen looked to the sky and saw Jesus standing at God's right hand. The people

rushed at him as one man, dragged him out
of the city, and began to stone him...
[Stephen] fell to his knees and cried out in a
loud voice, "Lord, do not hold this sin
against them." And with that he died.

Acts 7:57–60

Stephen's stoning illustrates how God brings good through the mistakes of humankind. This first martyrdom of a deeply spiritual man frightened the disciples of Jesus and caused them to scatter throughout the countryside of Judea and Samaria. That meant that even more people would hear about Jesus and expand the Christian church.

What does Stephen's stoning mean to present-day Christians? Is it merely a graphic example of primitive justice? These stonings were examples of early capital punishment. They were hands-on justice.

The community that condemned someone took part in the execution. Would that work today? Would you like to serve on a jury that not only condemned someone to death but took part in the execution of that person? Our faith as Christians calls us to forgive. Hopefully, taking part in an execution will never be required of us.

How do we react to modern-day holy persons who claim they see visions of God? Do we rush to cast hard words of disbelief (stones) at anyone who claims to see God? Before we cast stones of ridicule at others, we should remember that God loves all of us.

God of all, teach us to love others, especially those whom we do not understand. Stay our hands and lips when we would cast stones of disapproval at people whose religious practices are so different from ours. Forgive us for all the times we acted in haste and anger. In Jesus' name we pray. Amen.

Chapter 40
Living Stones

The First Epistle of Peter is a letter to scattered strangers, Gentile Christian communities in Asia Minor. These first Christians are addressed as new people of God, aliens in a pagan world. Among the varied instructions to live good lives of service, Peter, the Apostle of Jesus Christ, writes:

Come to him, a living stone, rejected by human beings but chosen and precious in the sight of God, and like living stones, let yourselves be built into a spiritual house, to be a holy priesthood, to offer spiritual sacrifices acceptable to God through Jesus Christ.

1 Peter 2:4, 5

What does it mean to be living stones? Believers joined by the Spirit to Christ the cornerstone, themselves become living stones that make up the spiritual church, the Christian community.

Living stones!

Envision a huge gathering of Christians, rock solid in faith, hands intertwined as they support the spiritual house of God! A multitude of voices lifted in prayer, thanksgiving, and song! How can mere mortals live out such a heavenly vision? It takes such strength and courage to become living stones. We could never manage it alone. But joined together, strengthened by the gifts of the Spirit, leaning on each other, we can become living stones.

How do we living stones promote the Kingdom of God? Peter's letter to his beloved scattered strangers gives five detailed chapters of instruction. Individual problems are addressed, including brotherly love, good example, growth in holiness, Christian charity, faithfulness and suffering. But the final sentence speaks volumes.

> **Greet one another with the embrace of true love. Peace to all of you who are in Christ.**
> **1 Peter 5:14**

We began this journey with hearts of stone. We explored many stone symbols in both the Old and the New Testament. Hopefully the Spirit of God has softened our stony hearts and infused us with warm hearts of flesh to love one another. Now, through continued prayer, meditation, and the gifts of the Spirit, we are urged to become living stones. We are sent out to spread the message of Christ's peace to all the world. Let us pray for the courage and strength to fulfill our mission.

O Spirit of God, gift us with the courage to be true living stones. Your generosity has enlivened our faith and strengthened our resolve. O Creator God, thank you for the sacrifices of your Son, Our Lord Jesus Christ. He is our cornerstone. Help us to support his mission of peace on earth. Teach us to become living stones, O God, in Jesus' name we pray. Amen.